Written by Diane Costa de Beauregard
Illustrated by Cyril Lepagnol

Specialist Adviser:
Yves Cohat
Marine Anthropologist

ISBN 0-944589-22-7
First U.S. Publication 1989 by
Young Discovery Library
217 Main St. • Ossining, NY 10562

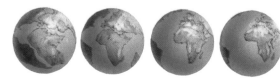

YOUNG DISCOVERY LIBRARY

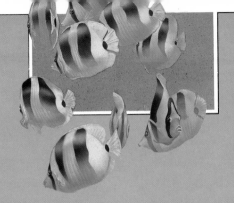

The Blue Planet: Seas & Oceans

YOUNG DISCOVERY LIBRARY

Imagine that you are looking at our planet from outer space. It would look blue! That is because Earth is covered by water over two-thirds of its surface.

This vast body of salt water is divided into five huge oceans and hundreds of smaller seas.

The largest, deepest and most dangerous ocean is the **Pacific.** Balboa, a Spanish explorer, misnamed it. He thought it was peaceful (pacific). The **Indian Ocean** borders India, Australia and Africa. The **Arctic** surrounds the North Pole and the **Antarctic** surrounds the South Pole.

Atlantic

Pacific

The **Atlantic Ocean** may be named
after Atlantis. Old stories say this is a
"lost continent" that sank in the sea.
Seas are smaller than oceans. Often
they are enclosed by land.

The top or surface of ocean waters
often change. Very rough in one
place and very calm in another.

The top of a volcano forms an island. Tiny animals, called coral, use calcium in the water to build walls around the island.

Another world, under the sea

For a long time, it was thought that the ocean floor was flat. Then people discovered mountains taller than any on land, vast plateaus, deep valleys and active volcanoes.

The echo sounder on a ship measures the ocean's depth. It sends a sound to the bottom and shows the time it takes to echo back to the surface.

Slowly, the island sinks, leaving behind the coral ring. Plants and trees grow on top. The shallow water in the middle is called a lagoon.

Some volcanoes rise above the water's surface to form islands. In the tropics, many of these will become coral rings called **atolls,** like the one in the pictures above.

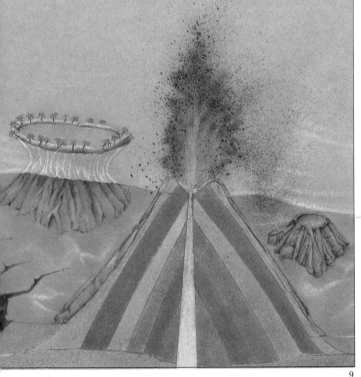

People have always dreamed of exploring the undersea world!

But you cannot go down without special equipment. You couldn't breathe, and the water's pressure would make your lungs feel squashed! In the 15th century, Leonardo da Vinci, who was a brilliant inventor as well as a painter, designed flippers, masks and breathing tubes. But they were not actually made until much later!

Many men tried to design an undersea attack boat for war. Many died in vain.

da Vinci's underwater gear

"The Turtle' (1776)

Helmet from the first diving suit, 1837

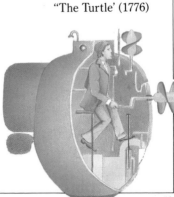

◄ In 1870 Jules Verne wrote a story about Captain Nemo and his amazing submarine.

Today, divers use tanks of compressed air. With tanks they can go deeper and stay longer under water.

Submarines can **descend** even deeper than divers. The Nautilus, a small French sub, can go down to 18,000 feet. In these great depths few plants grow and only strange sea life is found.

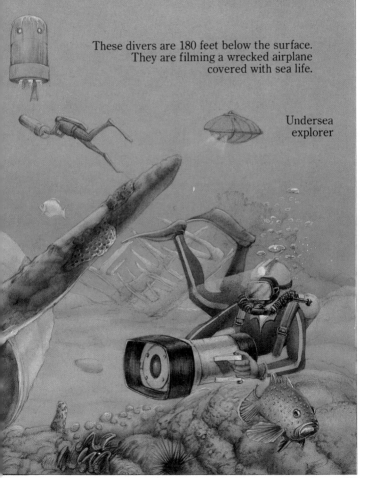

These divers are 180 feet below the surface. They are filming a wrecked airplane covered with sea life.

Undersea explorer

Every sea creature has its place in the food chain.
The chain starts with **plankton**, tiny specks of plant life (1) or animal life (2). This is food for small fish, like herring. Herring, in turn, make a tasty meal for a larger tuna. Then along comes a shark, who eats the tuna! Each fish is food for one bigger than itself. Shellfish gobble up the leftovers. The sea's 'garbage' is broken down, into minerals, which feed the plankton. The chain then starts all over again!

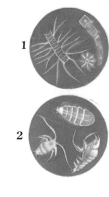

Fish like these live near the dark bottom of the sea.

15

The water may be warm or cold,
shallow or deep. Each area has
its own kinds of marine life.
**Around coral reefs the sea is
rich with life and color.**
The coral takes many shapes...
there are more than 2,500 kinds.

Green algae grows near the surface,
brown in the middle depths, and red
algae in deep water.

They may look like plants or
rocks. But the swirly things
you see here are animals! They
are sea **anemones** (ah-nem-o-nees).
Their venom is deadly to most
fish. Only the little clownfish
can hide in the anemone's tenta-
cles without danger. The orange
and white clown hides there and
finds scraps of food to eat!

Whales and dolphins
are mammals that
live in the sea.
They have lungs, like
humans, to breathe. They
must come up for air.
Their young are born
in the water and
always stay there.

Walruses,
like seals, have fur
coats. Part of their
time is spent in the
sea, part on land.
They rest and give
birth on land.

Seabirds, like
the gull, fly over
water to look for
fish. They can eat
and rest on the sea.

The gannet takes a 90-foot dive
for its dinner! It has a thick
skull with air pockets to protect
it from shock on hitting the water.

The Gulf Stream circles like the hands of a clock. Ships going to Europe use it to speed their trip. For the return the ships take a different way.

Currents and tides put the sea in motion.

Every day, the ocean rises at high tide and falls at low tide. The water is pulled by the power of the moon and sun. Currents are like rivers flowing in the ocean. They are created when winds blow and by the earth turning. The meeting of different waters makes currents: warm meets cold or fresh water meets salt.

The best known current is the Gulf Stream. This great body of warm water flows for thousands of miles. The winds that pass over it warm the land. But there are more fish in the cooler waters nearby.

Since ancient times, people have followed winds and currents. This Egyptian reed boat used both. ▶

This bird bobs up and down as a wave passes, but it is not carried along with the wave.

Winds blowing over the water create waves.

Waves rise and fall. They seem to push the water forward, but the water is not really moving. When there is a storm at sea, the wind can make waves taller than the largest ships. Such waves of foaming water have overturned many boats.

Some waves are born far from the shore.

Winds may create waves off our eastern coast. These are the same waves people will see rolling in, 3,000 miles away, in Europe!

Waves only stir things up on the water's surface.

A little further down, fish are swimming in calm water. There are some underwater currents, but these do not disturb boats.

When a storm arrives at high tide, look out for tidal waves!

These are giant waves that come without warning. Along our east coast they have caused much damage.

These globes show how the continents have drifted apart.
The globe on the left shows the earth 150 million years ago. The third globe is the earth today.
The last globe, on the right, shows how the earth will look in 50 million years.

In India, tidal waves have killed many thousands of people in floods.

But true tidal waves are not caused by storms or tides. They are set in motion by underwater earthquakes and volcanic eruptions. They occur so often in the Pacific Ocean, near Japan, that they have a Japanese name: tsunami. These waves are sometimes as tall as a ten-story building and can destroy many homes.

The Antarctic Ocean surrounds the South Pole.
Most of the world's penguins live here.

Polar bears live near the North Pole.
It is an area of ice and snow.

Most of this iceberg is underwater. It may take 2 to 4 years to melt.

Most of the earth's water is salty. **Almost all our fresh water is found at the North and South Poles, as ice.** Masses of ice are called glaciers. They move very slowly over the land towards the sea. Pieces of the glacier break off and fall into the water, forming **icebergs**. Until they, too, break up and melt, icebergs are a danger to ships. The **Titanic** was a famous ship that sank after hitting an iceberg. Today, ships use radar to warn of nearby icebergs.

Icebergs from the South Pole are flat on top.

Those from the North Pole look like jagged mountains.

We have to take care of the sea!

Look what happens when an oil tanker runs aground and breaks open, spilling oil into the sea. Some ships clean their storage tanks right in the water. Too many people seem to use the ocean as a garbage dump.

If this cormorant cannot clean the oil off its feathers, it will die.

If we throw our waste into the sea, we are poisoning the same fish that we catch for food! And we will not have clean beaches for swimming.

This type fishing boat is call
a trawler. It is dangerous wor
The men share the money earne

The sea provides us with food.
Fish is an important part of many
people's diets. Don't you enjoy
a tuna fish sandwich?

The fish are removed from the net and sorted (1), washed (2) and frozen (3).

This trawler is a floating factory! It drags a huge net, called a trawl, which catches fish as far down as 900 feet. These big ships are owned by large companies.

Undersea Oil

There are large amounts of
oil under the ocean floor.
Only some of it can be reached.
To get the oil, strong, steel
pumping rigs are built on
platforms. They must be able
to resist heavy winds and waves.

**Divers have collected pearls,
sponges and coral** for centuries.
They go down 20 feet or more,
holding their breath for up
to four minutes.

These may look like potatoes, but
they are nodules from the ocean floor.
Valuable minerals are in them.

There are metals in the sea.

All the earth's metals can be
found dissolved in sea water,
even gold! **Magnesium** is used
for building planes, and **bromide**
for photographic prints. At
this time only those two metals
are being taken from the sea.

Sponges are marine animals. They
are dried for use in homes.

Certain kinds of oysters hold pearls,
in great demand as jewelry.

The sea contains every shade of blue and green, and often silver and gray.

It is weather that changes the way the sea looks to us.

Green water means warm, shallow; rich in plankton and fish.

In heavy winds, the waves form whitecaps,
foamy tops like soap bubbles.

When it is cloudy, the sea is gray. When it
is sunny, it looks blue.

Far out the water is dark blue and there
are fewer fish.

The Sea

Behold the wonders of the mighty deep,
Where crabs and lobsters learn to creep,
And little fishes learn to swim,
And clumsy sailors tumble in.

Anonymous

Index